JUST A MINUTE MEDITATIONS

Finding God in Times of Depression

BY KATHRYN J. HERMES, FSP

Pauline
BOOKS & MEDIA
Boston

Library of Congress Control Number: 2024934297

ISBN 10: 0-8198-3471-8

ISBN 13: 978-0-8198-3471-3

Cover design by Tisa Muico

Published by Pauline Books & Media, 50 Saint Pauls Avenue, Boston, MA 02130-3491

Printed in the U.S.A.

www.pauline.org

Pauline Books & Media is the publishing house of the Daughters of St. Paul, an international congregation of women religious serving the Church with the communications media.

1 2 3 4 5 6 7 8 9 30 29 28 27 26 25 24

Contents

Introduction

Life has its seasons. The winter with its cold blasts, long darkness, and frozen snows melts into the first birdsongs of spring, when buds once more appear on the trees and children run and play. The black night of disappointment and the gloom of depression is one of those seasons that most, if not all, of us can expect to come and go in our lifetimes.

At times life takes us where we do not want to go: where we watch our horizons disappear, where we lose our world or loved ones who meant so much to us, where we convince ourselves we are no longer worthy of love, where our health fails us, where we simply feel down in the dumps and hopeless for some reason that escapes us, where we feel disappointed even by God. For me, a stroke when I was twenty-one melted into years of emotional struggles with the darkness and doubt that depression brings. When we are despondent, it may seem that the seasons have stopped, that the gentle breezes of spring will never again bless our life. It is when our life seems frozen in discouragement that we most need to know we are not alone. We long for the warmth and assurance of Jesus' tender care.

When we suffer with depression, finding words to share with the Lord what is troubling our heart can seem almost impossible. Is there a way to hear his voice? To trust his heart?

These short meditations you hold in your hand will offer you courage at this unsettling time. When you have no words, these pages will provide them. When the voices you hear in your heart are harsh, listening to God speak his promises will stretch you to trust once more in Jesus, in yourself, and in the future. Taking time to ponder, to wait upon the Lord, and to speak with him about your struggles will increase your capacity to receive his unconditional love and to recognize his nearness to you through it all. Your frequent recourse to the One who loves you forever will renew your spirit.

This short booklet of meditation and prayer, when combined with other types of care and treatment, could be considered a lifeline. At one moment it may be for you the first step out of the swirling darkness into the light of trust in God's loving care. At another it may be the resource you keep with you for when you need a pick-me-up. These words of hope will challenge the grinding discouragement and desolation on those days when you just can't seem to shake free of the sadness. You will find this little book a useful companion for deeper prayer when beginning or ending the day, or while spending time with Jesus in the Eucharist in adoration.

Here is an easy method for reading these meditations. It will unlock in your heart the courage to believe in God's desire to save and bless you even through the darkest hours of your life:

1. The meditations start at the beginning of the journey through depression and walk with you toward wholeness and peace. If this is the first meditation and prayer guide you are using on depression, I encourage you to read the meditations in order. However, there are times when God will lead you to pray with certain meditations. Go wherever God leads you.
2. Before you read, stop and remember a moment when someone delighted in having you around. Tell God how grateful you are for that gift of love.
3. Begin to read the meditation. Talk to God about what is burdening you right now. Then reread the words of Scripture in the meditation, hearing them as if God were speaking to you by name. Even place your name right in the passage

and imagine God speaking these words to you directly. Notice what that is like and tell God how grateful you are.

4. Move gently to the short prayer that concludes the meditation and, if it helps you draw closer to God, use one of the prayers in the section at the end of the book. These prayers, some written by persons who themselves have walked through dark valleys and some found in Scripture, can give you the words you are searching for as you lift your heart to God's own heart and seek to soak in his inconceivable love for you.

Sometimes, depression is more than passing blues that come and go depending on the events of our lives. Persistent feelings of depression may be accompanied by problems with sleep, appetite, concentration, energy, or negative thoughts, or by the loss of interest in or ability to enjoy activities. If you experience these symptoms, I encourage you to seek the advice of a mental health practitioner to assess how the combining of different modalities can bring you greater relief and strengthen you in your journey to wholeness.

Depression cannot be "prayed away." Depression, whether mild or debilitating, creates a host of symptoms that can affect nearly all aspects of life and functioning. Yet prayer, when combined with other suitable and appropriate resources for wholeness and mental health, has always been the strength of God's people in their every sorrow.

Dear reader, wherever you are in this journey of life, whatever hurts, whatever weighs on your heart, don't go it alone. When you pray with the word of God you are united to the millions of people who have prayed and reflected on God's love and tenderness for thousands of years. Most especially, in those quiet moments God is with you in a special way. You are never alone. I pray you will find calm and quiet for your soul.

1

You Want to Know Our Pain

And she gave birth to her firstborn son and wrapped him in bands of cloth, and laid him in a manger, because there was no place for them in the inn.

In that region there were shepherds living in the fields, keeping watch over their flock by night. Then an angel of the Lord stood before them, and the glory of the Lord shone around them, and they were terrified. But the angel said to them, "Do not be afraid; for see—I am bringing you good news of great joy for all the people: to you is born this day in the city of David a Savior."

LUKE 2:7–11

Brokenness, dashed expectations, and awful times can enter unbidden into our life. They may leave us with such sadness that the tears never seem to stop. Or we may feel numb, empty, paralyzed. No matter what our experience, depression is terribly heavy, and the heart's storms can weigh us down.

The cosmic reality, however—the one thing that makes an eternal difference for each of us—is that Jesus set aside the glory of heaven to share our life. Into our broken world, Love was born. When he saw us cry, he too wept. When he saw us burdened with weakness and wandering from our losses, he pointed out the way and carried our burdens with us.

Whenever sadness sneaks up on you, or if you are in that dark place right now, remember that Jesus is walking with you through it all.

Jesus, never leave me!

2

You Are About to Do a New Thing

Thus says the Lord,
your Redeemer, the Holy One of Israel. . . .
I am about to do a new thing;
now it springs forth, do you not perceive it?
I will make a way in the wilderness.

Isaiah 43:14, 19

In the Scriptures God speaks to his people. In passages such as this one from the prophet Isaiah, we hear what God's voice is like. Praying with the words of God in the Scriptures, we can learn to recognize his voice in all areas of our lives. When we ache, God speaks words of hope. When we cry out in the pitch dark, begging for our life, God speaks to us through friends, songs, a book, a pastor.

What is breaking your heart right now? A deep disappointment? Regret over the past? Defeat and the humiliation of failure? Loss and grief? Words heard long ago that still control you?

Right now, let Jesus speak to your heart: "Come, it's all right. Come to me exactly as you are. Come even if everything is not okay. Even if you feel as if the world is too much for you. My arms are open; come to me. See, I am doing a new thing."

Jesus, I feel like I am in the wilderness. What is the new thing you are bringing about for me?

3

Come to My Rescue

> A windstorm arose on the sea, so great that the boat was being swamped by the waves; but [Jesus] was asleep. And they went and woke him up, saying, "Lord, save us! We are perishing!" And he said to them, "Why are you afraid, you of little faith?" Then he got up and rebuked the winds and the sea; and there was a dead calm. They were amazed, saying, "What sort of man is this, that even the winds and the sea obey him?"
>
> MATTHEW 8:24–27

The apostles were experienced fishermen, familiar with the weather patterns on the Sea of Galilee. Yet they were so unnerved by the sudden squall that they feared they were going to drown. Tempests have a way of sneaking up on us also. Sometimes the turmoil can swamp our fragile hearts, flooding us with anxiety. In the turbulence we might have the illusion that we are in this alone—that making it through depends entirely upon our strategy and skill. The apostles remind us how important it is to call out to Jesus for help.

Paradoxically, it was only when the apostles lost the control they *thought* they had over their lives that they discovered the authority Jesus exercised over the storms that threatened them. We don't have to face the overwhelming waves of depression alone. Jesus is with us in the boat; even if he seems to be sleeping, the winds and the seas of our heart will obey him.

Lord, save me. The storm is frightening, and the waves are high. Come to my rescue!

4

Lord, Hear My Cry for Help

In my distress I called upon the LORD;
    to my God I cried for help.
From his temple he heard my voice,
    and my cry to him reached his ears. . . .
He bowed the heavens, and came down. . . .
He reached down from on high, he took me;
    he drew me out of mighty waters.

PSALM 18:6, 9, 16

In our relationship with God even distress has meaning. It is often in the wounded places of our lives that he bows the heavens and comes down, reaches down and grabs us, drawing us out of mighty waters.

That's usually not how we think about our problems when we are trudging through dark valleys. Intrusive thoughts may disturb our peace: *I have failed. I have no value. My views are worthless. All this is my fault. I don't know what is happening to me. Why do I feel this way?*

Praying Psalm 18 gives us hope in the suffering seasons. It reminds us to hold together distress and hope, to cling to belief even when all seems lost.

Though you may be surrounded by churning waters, God is still greater. Even now he is reaching down to draw you up out of the storm.

O God, strong and faithful, reach down from heaven and save me!

5

Help Me to See You Walking with Me

> As [Jesus] approached the gate of the town, a man who had died was being carried out. He was his mother's only son, and she was a widow; and with her was a large crowd from the town. When the Lord saw her, he had compassion for her.
>
> LUKE 7:12–13

When we live at the edge of hope, when we've lost what is dearest to our heart, when we've reached the end of the horizon and there is nowhere else to go, we know in our spirit a mourning so deep it seems it will never go away. What had been a happy life becomes a dark journey, and with a frightened heart we trudge through the fog.

Our culture tells us to avoid the suffering that comes with loss, offering a thousand ways to anesthetize the pain. Instead, we will find our way through depression only by facing the anguish with Jesus, who has great compassion for us.

Imagine Jesus walking into places in your life that seem to have died. Choose an image that symbolizes the misery and offer it to him. Keep your eyes fixed on Jesus and ask him what he wants you to know and understand about all this. Let him be with you.

Gentle Jesus, these places in my life frighten me. I trust in you, my only hope.

6

Lord, Lift My Heart

For it was you who formed my inward parts;
    you knit me together in my mother's womb.
I praise you, for I am fearfully and wonderfully made.
    Wonderful are your works;
that I know very well.
    My frame was not hidden from you,
when I was being made in secret,
    intricately woven in the depths of the earth.

PSALM 139:13–15

We each experience depression differently. Some have no appetite; others can't sleep. Some feel that life has no meaning, that there is no future for them; others experience their trust in themselves shattered and walk with fearful steps into each day. We may also experience many physical symptoms, such as unexplained aches or pains, headaches, cramps, or digestive problems.

It is difficult, at these times, to "praise God, for we are fearfully and wonderfully made." We look in the mirror and don't like the person we see. We feel disappointment in circumstances we didn't expect and isolation from friends and family. It is a tender place.

When we ache for normalcy but find ourselves in the land of suffering where everything we knew and long for has been taken away, we may begin to appreciate the smallest things: sunrises, a pet, a cup of coffee, a few moments of quiet prayer. With time we discover how resilient we have become and how amazing we creatures of God can be. Truly then, even in the misery, we taste the sweetness of this psalm.

I praise you, Lord, for I am fearfully and wonderfully made.

7

Jesus, Help Me Breathe

> For wisdom is . . . a breath of the power of God,
> and a pure emanation of the glory of the Almighty;
> therefore nothing defiled gains entrance into her.
> For she is a reflection of eternal light,
> a spotless mirror of the working of God,
> and an image of his goodness.
>
> WISDOM 7:24–26

The story of creation tells us that God breathed into us the breath of life. From that primordial moment, breath has been the thread that runs through our days. The way we breathe reflects how we are reacting to situations and conditions around us and within our inner world. Shallow breaths, quick breaths, deep breaths. . . . When we repetitively revisit the memories that haunt us about parts of our life that we can't change, we are probably breathing very shallowly. Like mice in a maze, our memories are running through predictable programs, unable to escape the stories we are telling ourselves.

Every corner our imagination turns, hope seems boxed in and the future shut out.

In one way, you could say, our life tells its story through our breath.

Calming your nervous system by slowing your breathing can create just the tiniest crack by which you can relaunch your hope. So, take a deep breath, slow your mind down, and in that space of silence invite God's loving tenderness to fill you.

Breathing in, I hear you call me by name. Breathing out, I whisper, "I trust you, my Lord and Savior."

8

Jesus, Remind Me Who I Am

> Then Jesus went with them to a place called Gethsemane; and he said to his disciples, "Sit here while I go over there and pray." He took with him Peter and the two sons of Zebedee, and began to be grieved and agitated. Then he said to them, "I am deeply grieved, even to death; remain here, and stay awake with me." And going a little farther, he threw himself on the ground and prayed, "My Father, if it is possible, let this cup pass from me; yet not what I want but what you want." Then he came to the disciples and found them sleeping.
>
> Matthew 26:36–40

Few experiences expose us to our own vulnerability as sharply as having to walk through the darkness of life's journey without others at our side. In the garden that witnessed his agony, we see that Jesus had entrusted himself to people who would not be there for him in the anguished moment he most needed them.

So many in our lonely age are afflicted with the heartache of not belonging, of having been forgotten or excluded. There is a unique inner torment when we feel left outside and unremembered by family, friends, society, the Church. At these times when, like Jesus, we truly are alone with our God, we can take our stand beside him in the Garden of Gethsemane, to comfort him and be comforted by him in a misery we both share.

Jesus, my Brother, when I feel alone, remind me who I am: a child of the Father. Fill me with your Spirit so I can say with you, "Abba, Father."

9

O Lord, My Soul Cries Out to You

> But I, O Lord, cry out to you;
> in the morning my prayer comes before you.
> O Lord, why do you cast me off?
> Why do you hide your face from me?
> Wretched and close to death from my youth up,
> I suffer your terrors; I am desperate.
>
> Psalm 88:13–15

To me, the most moving passages of Scripture are the prayers of doubt and incomprehension that we find in the Psalms. "O Lord, why do you cast me off? Where are you? I need you desperately, but are you listening? Do you even care?" God is not put off by a desolate heart's cry. When we are at our wit's end, our heart's pleading is itself a prayer. Even more, the frustration we feel at not being able to connect with God reveals the very strength of our desire.

In whatever way you can, reach out to God. In the morning, let your cry come to him. When the pangs of loneliness tear at your heart, reach out to him. When anxiety makes you feel like your soul will shatter, breathe deeply and whisper Jesus' name. When you trudge home alone while others are at the pub with friends, remind him how much you are suffering. When the night is endless and sleep eludes you, take a moment to sit in front of a sacred image. Staying in the moment and reaching out to God is a very precious form of prayer.

O Lord, I lift up my heart to you.

10

Jesus, I Want to See!

> Some people brought a blind man to him and begged him to touch him. He took the blind man by the hand and led him out of the village; and when he had put saliva on his eyes and laid his hands on him, he asked him, "Can you see anything?" And the man looked up and said, "I can see people, but they look like trees, walking." Then Jesus laid his hands on his eyes again; and he looked intently and his sight was restored, and he saw everything clearly.
>
> MARK 8:22–26

Depression is an invitation to slow down and take stock of our blindness. Some of us may have been blind to the way that choices made earlier in life now seem to box us in. We no longer feel that we are flourishing, fruitful, or effective. For others, a passage through the doldrums might help us see there is more that God wants to give us now. It eventually becomes a journey of awakened spiritual desire. For still others, depression is helped best by also talking out these issues with a professional. No doubt, for most of us it's a unique combination of all three.

This passage reminds us that even when we feel befuddled and confused, Jesus sees us! We are assured that even if it is not yet possible to see clearly the purpose of what we are enduring, our blindness will be healed in time. Jesus' work in us is unspectacular, steady, unhurried, but sure.

Lord Jesus, Divine Healer, I want to see you!

11
By Which You Have Saved Me

> When you pass through the waters, I will be with you;
> and through the rivers, they shall not overwhelm you;
> when you walk through fire you shall not be burned,
> and the flame shall not consume you.
>
> Isaiah 43:2

When we find ourselves in situations we can't manage, when we are in over our head with problems, when all we've built is left in ashes, Jesus promises us that we will not be harmed. It is then that we may ask God, "Where were you when the rivers were overwhelming *me*, when *I* most needed protection, security, and love?"

On one retreat afternoon, I wanted to make sure that Jesus realized how tough some situations in my life had been. "Do you see this?" I asked him. In my heart I heard the words, "By which I have saved you." That was a disconcerting response. "Well, what about this other thing?" "By which I have saved you." The voice seemed calm and patient. Not to be deterred, I tried one more time and pointed out the most devastating experience. Again came the quiet reply, "By which I have saved you."

Although I felt that I had walked through some of the darkest valleys of my life, I realized that God was telling me that he had always been at my side. This response of God might seem harsh, but over many years I have come to trust that healing is always a combination of taking care of ourselves and having confidence that God is taking care of us.

Through all I have endured, O Lord, you have saved me.

12
The Lord Is My Shepherd

The LORD is my shepherd, I shall not want.
    He makes me lie down in green pastures;
he leads me beside still waters;
    he restores my soul. . . .
You prepare a table before me. . . .
Surely goodness and mercy shall follow me
    all the days of my life,
and I shall dwell in the house of the LORD
    my whole life long.

PSALM 23:1–3A, 5–6

In the wilderness, sheep are in constant danger from prowling predators and dependent on their shepherd for everything. This psalm conjures up images of a verdant wilderness, abundance of grain and new life, a safe refuge from danger.

The psalmist proclaims that the Lord prepares a "table" in this wilderness. The Israelites had doubted that God could provide for them as they left Egypt and encountered for the first time the possibility of having nothing to eat. Perhaps we too wonder if God will provide for us when the desert sands are hot and the journey of depression long.

Jesus the Good Shepherd leads us into his house where we may dwell our whole life long. He lays out for us the table of the Eucharist, where his goodness and mercy meet us whenever we approach him in Holy Communion.

What are the ways God has shepherded you in the wilderness? How has he led you into the desert, like the Israelites of old, to teach you that only your Shepherd can satisfy your deepest longings?

Jesus, Shepherd, Savior, Merciful Brother, Divine Compassion, have mercy on me.

13

You, O Lord, Call Me by Name

Now he was teaching in one of the synagogues on the Sabbath. And just then there appeared a woman with a spirit that had crippled her for eighteen years. She was bent over and was quite unable to stand up straight. When Jesus saw her, he called her over and said, "Woman, you are set free from your ailment." When he laid his hands on her, immediately she stood up straight and began praising God.

LUKE 13:10–13

For eighteen years—maybe more than half her life—this woman so bent and crippled had been staring at the ground. She was isolated from everyone around her as they talked over her, around her, about her.

I often imagine what it must have been like for her to hear a voice that spoke to her with such gentleness that Sabbath day. What was in her heart as she crossed the floor of the synagogue toward Jesus as everyone looked on? Though others may not have noticed her except when she was in their way, Jesus had always seen her. Her neighbors might not have wanted to get involved. After all, eighteen years is a very long time to care about someone who's ill. Jesus, however, reached out to her with the gift of new life.

For those of us who suffer with depression, the months and years of illness could seem interminable. We, too, might feel bent over under the weight of all we bear. Yet we, like this woman, are seen by Jesus.

Jesus, you who know everything about me, let me hear you call my name.

14

Jesus, Help Me to Hope

> For surely I know the plans I have for you, says the LORD, plans for your welfare and not for harm, to give you a future with hope.
>
> JEREMIAH 29:11

Plans for my welfare? Are you kidding? After all that has happened to me? Are you saying that everything that has gone wrong is actually part of a plan? That the harm I have endured has been some kind of blessing?

When I first encountered the above proclamation from God through the prophet Jeremiah, I was jolted out of the kind of thoughts that had begun to shape my life. All I could do was surrender my mind, my will, and my heart, and hope it was true. Now, forty years later, I know it is true. I now can see that even the most vulnerable places, even the years that brought the greatest anguish, had been woven by God into his plan for my welfare. Those places and years did not harm me. Yes, they were hard. Yes, sometimes they broke me. Yes, I cannot deny that they had lifelong consequences. Yes, I have had to struggle because of them. But yes, in some mysterious way, I now know that they belong in my life.

When we find a Scripture passage that speaks to us this strongly, we need to cherish it, for it will nourish us throughout our life. It may take decades until we can say from our own experience that we absolutely know that it is true. Each step of faith along the way, however, is valuable. God will not deceive.

God my Father, I rest my heart in your hands. I trust you. Lead me.

15

Listen to Jesus

> Great crowds assembled to listen to him and to be cured of their ailments.
>
> LUKE 5:15 (NABRE)

At the time of Jesus, the Jewish people in Judea were under Roman domination. Tensions and uprisings were frequent. Divisions, conflict, poverty, social injustice, and economic disparity made life difficult. There is something all too familiar about this reality. It is our own. As we watch the unfolding of horrific events jeopardizing the lives and fortunes of our sisters and brothers with whom we share this planet, we might despair that our own lives might also spin out of control.

It is crucial to pay close attention to what we allow to enter our mind and heart. Where do we get our information from? Who are the people we are sorting out life with?

The crowds recognized that Jesus had something to offer them that no other person, government, or policy could. They gathered around him simply to listen. Jesus reveals to us something more real and enduring than the passing power of government authorities and military strategies. In Christ, God's kingdom is already unfolding. Nothing can stop it. Nothing can ultimately harm us.

So put down your phone, disconnect from social media for a time, check a reliable source of news no more than once a day, and with all that saved time, come before Jesus in the Eucharist and listen.

I cast my cares upon you, Jesus, right now. I trust you to care for me.

16

Jesus Knows Where I Am Hiding

When it was evening on that day, the first day of the week, and the doors of the house where the disciples had met were locked for fear of the Jews, Jesus came and stood among them and said, "Peace be with you." After he said this, he showed them his hands and his side. Then the disciples rejoiced when they saw the Lord.

JOHN 20:19–20

The disciples were huddled in a locked room, riddled with fear, hiding. We've all been there. We don't want anyone to know about the troubles we bear: that we aren't perfectly put together; that we feel responsible for not belonging, not getting ahead, not being included, not being significant. And so we hide. Jesus breaks into the places of our solitude, just as he did with the apostles after the unimaginable horror of his crucifixion and the resplendent glory of his resurrection. And there, Jesus showed them his own wounds.

You may cower in fear because you feel deeply wounded by the way your life has played out. Invite Jesus into that place. Hear him say to you and to everyone else who was a part of what brought you pain, "Peace be with you. Peace be with you all."

Risen Jesus, walk through the walls I've put up around my wounds. Show me your hands and side still bearing the wounds of our salvation.

17

Let Your Face Shine on Us, O Lord!

> There are many who say, "O that we might see some
>   good!
>   Let the light of your face shine on us, O LORD!"
> I will both lie down and sleep in peace;
>   for you alone, O LORD, make me lie down in safety.
>
> PSALM 4:6, 8

When the world's news is more than we can bear and the brokenness of the human heart is writ large across the globe, we might turn to prayer, asking God to let his face shine on us. It's not so easy, however, to lie down and fall peacefully asleep. The "what if's" take over in the night hours, and we toss and turn with restless worries. The surge of feelings can quickly overwhelm our faith.

In a particularly difficult time, my mother had to support me with her own faith. On a telephone call after 9/11, she could sense my spiraling emotions, and she said clearly and firmly, "Kathryn, God is present! God is here! God is taking care of you."

When we suffer with depression, we are particularly vulnerable to negative news. Headlines and social media magnify the psychological strain we are already under. When we can't lie down and sleep in peace, when we can't think ourselves into feeling safe, we may need to rely on another's faith. At these times, it helps to reach out to someone we trust, to ask them to share their faith. Then just hold on.

O Lord, help me sleep in peace. Help me to realize that right now I am safe.

18

You Love Even the Messy Parts of My Life

Who will separate us from the love of Christ? Will hardship, or distress, or persecution, or famine, or nakedness, or peril, or sword? . . . I am convinced that neither death, nor life, nor angels, nor rulers, nor things present, nor things to come, nor powers, nor height, nor depth, nor anything else in all creation, will be able to separate us from the love of God in Christ Jesus our Lord.

ROMANS 8:35, 38–39

God loves you. That is the whole story. God's love is where it all began. God's love sustains us no matter what. God's love sanctifies us. God's love forgives us again and again. God's love will receive us one day when we pass from this life into eternity. God's love is everything, and nothing has the power to cut us off from this love.

On this earth the experience of unconditional love is not fully possible. We dream of it, but we never arrive at offering such incredible love to another or receiving it ourselves. We love to the extent that we can in each season of our life. The heartbreak and the shame of having failed in love might tempt us to give up on ourselves. We might even wonder, "How could God love someone like me?"

Jesus doesn't step away from any part of your story. Instead, precisely in what you regret most—the decisions you feel most guilty about, the losses that cloud your heart with gloom—he moves closer to restore you.

Your love washes over me, O Lord.

19

Jesus, I Want to Be Well

> Jesus went up to Jerusalem. . . . [A] man was there who had been ill for thirty-eight years. When Jesus saw him lying there and knew that he had been there a long time, he said to him, "Do you want to be made well?"
>
> JOHN 5:1, 5–6

Jesus has an endless desire to be a part of our life. Again and again, he seeks us out and asks us this question: "Do you want to be made well? Do you want a life healed and whole?" And Jesus will respect your response.

Saying yes to this journey toward restoration may be the riskiest "yes" you will ever say in your life. It takes courage to hope for healing and to look into the eyes of Jesus, who wants you once again to flourish. One day you will look back on the first tentative and brave steps you took and bless the day you began to surrender everything into the hands of the Divine Healer.

Hear these words addressed by Jesus to you: "Do you trust me? Can you have confidence that I will make you well? Even if I restore you in ways that you have not envisioned, do you still want to let me make you well?"

Say yes. This is the longest yes you will ever say, because it starts from this moment and will be repeated every moment until you walk the streets of the New Jerusalem.

Yes, Jesus. I want to be well. Give me courage today, courage for the next step with you at my side.

20

Help Me Trust Your Promise

> Truly, O people in Zion, inhabitants of Jerusalem, you shall weep no more. . . . Though the Lord may give you the bread of adversity and the water of affliction, yet your Teacher will not hide himself any more. . . . On every lofty mountain and every high hill there will be brooks running with water . . . on the day when the LORD binds up the injuries of his people, and heals the wounds inflicted by his blow.
>
> ISAIAH 30:19–20, 25–26

Reading and trusting this promise found in the prophet Isaiah assures us that what appears to us as disintegration is, mysteriously, a graced offer of divine restructuring. The Lord loves us too much to leave us as we are. In this uncomfortable place we stand on a threshold, for we are no longer who we were and not quite yet who we are becoming.

God proves his love for us by his fidelity to us in this "in between" space: no matter how lonely, messed up, or shattered we may feel our lives have become, God is still faithfully breathing life into us.

Open yourself to the mysterious way the Lord will bind up your injuries and heal your wounds. Ask God to show you who you are becoming with the power of his gracious love.

God, help me trust your promise that when this night lifts, "the light of the sun will be sevenfold" (Is 30:26).

21

Lord, You Know That I Love You

> When they had finished breakfast, Jesus said to Simon Peter, "Simon son of John. . . . Do you love me?" And he said to him, "Lord, you know everything; you know that I love you."
>
> JOHN 21:15, 17

Warming himself by a fire in the night, Peter had betrayed the Lord. Now, beside another charcoal fire, Peter proclaims his love with humbled heart. On the night of Jesus' arrest, after Peter had protested that he didn't even know Jesus, guilt must have tormented him. Now by this fire in the quiet morning, peace and mercy flow as he experiences Jesus' love and trust.

When we suffer with depression, guilt can be tricky. Perhaps we feel guilty for being depressed, or we become depressed because we don't know how to deal with our guilt.

When we remember the wreckage our choices have created in our lives or in the lives of others, we need to do so in humble conversation *with* Jesus. The Evil One is more than happy to bring up memories of everything we now regret. His voice is recognizable because it is accusatory and fills us with shame. His purpose is to separate us from Jesus, to make us afraid of being near him and doubtful of his mercy.

Jesus wants you to let him be at your side, no matter what you've done in your life. He only wants to know one thing: "Do you love me?"

Yes, Lord, you know everything about me. You know that I love you.

22
A New Treasure Is Being Revealed

"Do not store up for yourselves treasures on earth, where moth and rust consume and where thieves break in and steal; but store up for yourselves treasures in heaven, where neither moth nor rust consumes and where thieves do not break in and steal. For where your treasure is, there your heart will be also."

MATTHEW 6:19–21

Why did this happen? Our plans were perfect. . . . Everything was ready to go. . . . We were so happy. . . . We were doing everything right. . . .

We can plague ourselves with thoughts of the way things should be, could be. But maybe the plans that seemed so perfect were not the actual plan at all. Maybe they were the plan for a season of our life, or simply for a single chapter, and now the page has turned. A new season is being revealed.

The blueprint of our life offers a succession of "treasures," all in some clear or cloudy way pointing to eternal treasure. When we get used to one treasure we are like children: we don't want to let it go. All sorts of distorted reasons and negative emotions accompany our attempts to hold on to what we have.

Are your thought patterns and expectations closing you off from the possibility of something different? But meanwhile, is someone or something offering you a new direction?

What's holding you back?

Jesus, I lean my forehead against yours. Quiet my heart. Still my mind. Help me trust the future. Make me yearn for you, my everlasting and eternal Treasured One.

23

How Beautiful It Is to Praise You

Praise the LORD!
How good it is to sing praises to our God;
for he is gracious, and a song of praise is fitting.
The LORD builds up Jerusalem;
he gathers the outcasts of Israel.
He heals the brokenhearted,
and binds up their wounds.
He determines the number of the stars;
he gives to all of them their names.
Great is our Lord, and abundant in power;
his understanding is beyond measure.

PSALM 147:1–5

The way the Lord cares for his people, as described in this psalm, is gentle *and* powerful. As this psalm indicates, God knows every need of his people. He tenderly gathers them together. His careful eye notices where they are broken, what burdens they carry, what healing they need. He binds up all their wounds. This is why a song of praise is fitting.

God's action is why we can believe that our tomorrows will be different from our yesterdays. When we believe in what *God* makes possible in our lives, we are on the way to seeing everything that has been broken transformed into something beautiful.

Whether depression is a new experience or your broken heart is on the mend, sing with courage your praise to the Lord, for, as the Liturgy affirms, it is everywhere and in all things right and just to praise him.

O Lord, how beautiful it is to praise you. Always and everywhere I will give you thanks.

24

You Are the God of My Salvation

Though the fig tree does not blossom,
    and no fruit is on the vines;
though the produce of the olive fails
    and the fields yield no food;
though the flock is cut off from the fold
    and there is no herd in the stalls,
yet I will rejoice in the LORD;
    I will exult in the God of my salvation.
GOD, the Lord, is my strength;
    he makes my feet like the feet of a deer,
    and makes me tread upon the heights.

HABAKKUK 3:17–19

We sometimes gauge God's goodness by the circumstances of our life. When God doesn't answer our prayers or provide for us in the way we ask him to, the disappointment can be crushing. We might even doubt that God hears our pleas at all. In the above passage, the prophet Habakkuk describes a worst-case scenario: no fruit, no harvest, no flocks . . . no food, no security, no future. Imagine the panic we would feel in that situation! But Habakkuk declares: "yet I will rejoice in the Lord." His faith is not in what he sees in the world around him, but in who God declares himself to be. Even if the circumstances in his life do not change, he will yet find his strength in God.

No matter the tragedy, anxiety, or sorrow that troubles you, the God who gives you breath is faithful. He will give you "the feet of a deer": graceful and swift, surefooted in your reliance on him, undeterred by situations that would normally get you down.

God, give me the grace, courage, and inner strength to live victoriously.

25

O Give Thanks to the Lord

O give thanks to the Lord, for he is good,
  for his steadfast love endures forever . . .
who alone does great wonders,
  for his steadfast love endures forever.

Psalm 136:1, 4

The psalms give us words for praising God that have been used for thousands of years. Meditating on and praying with these words increases our capacity for gratitude and takes the edge off depression. Then we begin to move through life with a certain graciousness, more mindful of unexpected blessings and simple things like waking up in the morning, drinking a glass of water, or feeling a cool breeze brush across our face. Negative thoughts are more easily shaken off. The sense of being accompanied through life's unpredictability makes us smile. Slowly we begin to marvel at the reliability of God's goodness despite life's inevitable pain. We see that there is a beauty to having lived at all.

In a litany of gratitude, Psalm 136 praises God for his glory and enumerates the ways in which he has remembered the Chosen People and rescued them through his power. Praying with this psalm reminds us to stop resurfacing thoughts of hopelessness, fear, and doubt. Recalling the ways in which God has been there for others and for ourselves brings us peace.

I thank you, O Lord, for your steadfast love endures forever.

26

We Are Children of the Resurrection

> The angel said to the women, "Do not be afraid; I know that you are looking for Jesus who was crucified. He is not here; for he has been raised, as he said. Come, see the place where he lay. Then go quickly and tell his disciples, 'He has been raised from the dead, and indeed he is going ahead of you to Galilee; there you will see him.' This is my message for you."
>
> MATTHEW 28:5–7

Christ is the Victorious One who in his death and resurrection conquered evil. No longer is there death that cannot bring life, pain that cannot generate fullness, sadness that cannot be transformed into deep joy. There are no limitations, fragilities, psychological wounds, or mood disorders stronger than the Resurrected One.

Through Baptism we are conformed to the image of Christ and made children of the victory of the resurrection. In the Eucharist, all of the salvific power of the death and resurrection of the Savior is made available to us. Jesus lives in us now.

And so, if you keep faith, if you keep loving and hoping through the tears, then the joy of the resurrection, the glory of the God who is with you, will guide you through sorrow into a calm and blissful respite where you may bask in the assurance of his tender care.

Lord, though this earth is a vale of tears, I have confidence that sorrow will not have the last word, because I belong to you who have already conquered death. This is my faith.

27

Remember This Sign of God's Love

> Remember the long way that the LORD your God has led you these forty years in the wilderness. . . . The clothes on your back did not wear out and your feet did not swell these forty years. . . . [T]he LORD your God is bringing you into a good land, a land with flowing streams, with springs and underground waters welling up in valleys and hills, a land of wheat and barley, of vines and fig trees and pomegranates, a land of olive trees and honey.
>
> DEUTERONOMY 8:2, 4, 7–8

One of the most beautiful gifts we can receive from God as we heal is the gift of remembering and reverencing the past with wonder and amazement.

As the Israelites stand on the border of the Promised Land, this is what Moses hopes the people will remember: *Although it has been tough to wander in the desert these past forty years, as you look back you can see that your shoes didn't wear out and your feet didn't swell.* That is what could be expected for people traveling in sweltering heat year after year: disintegrating shoes and tired feet. And yet in these particular ways, the Lord in his compassion has provided for them.

When you think about the parts of your life's pilgrimage that have been marked with emotional pain, what memories surface? Once you can see a way that God has provided for you throughout the tough parts of your journey, hold that memory with reverence.

My God, may I gratefully and forever cherish the signs of your love for me.

28

You Change My Sorrow into Praise

Sing aloud, O daughter Zion;
    shout, O Israel!
Rejoice and exult with all your heart,
    O daughter Jerusalem! . . .
The king of Israel, the LORD, is in your midst;
    you shall fear disaster no more.
On that day it shall be said to Jerusalem:
Do not fear, O Zion;
    do not let your hands grow weak.
The LORD, your God, is in your midst,
    a warrior who gives victory;
he will rejoice over you with gladness,
    he will renew you in his love;
he will exult over you with loud singing
    as on a day of festival.

ZEPHANIAH 3:14, 15B–18A

Even as we heal, we may still struggle to believe in our own goodness. Zephaniah ends his prophecies about the suffering and difficulties of Israel with an alternating chorus of exuberant gladness. First, the prophet invites the people to sing aloud, to shout, to rejoice, to exult with all their heart. Then he reveals the words of the Lord, who breaks out in song, who rejoices, who dances with gladness over his people.

Now sing with Zephaniah: God dances for joy because of *me*! God delights in *me*. God rests his love on *me*. "Have no more fear," is the divine song God sings over you, "for I am here." Keep walking, reaching, expecting, believing.

I rejoice, for you change my sorrow into praise!

29

You Alone Have Guided Me

He sustained him in a desert land,
        in a howling wilderness waste;
he shielded him, cared for him,
        guarded him as the apple of his eye.
As an eagle stirs up its nest,
        and hovers over its young;
as it spreads its wings, takes them up,
        and bears them aloft on its pinions,
the LORD alone guided him.

DEUTERONOMY 32:10–12A

Depression certainly can feel like a desert expanse that turns our life inside out and upside down. Do you remember the beginning of your journey into the numbing emptiness, not knowing how you would make it through? Take a moment to look back with the eyes of faith. Though God may not have removed you from situations of pain, he has shielded, cared for, and guarded you with tremendous love and affection.

The passage from Deuteronomy describes God's love for you through the image of a mother eagle. The eagle is not content to leave her young in the comfortable nest: she knows that something greater awaits them if they take the risk and start to fly. She begins to break the nest apart so the eaglets will have no choice but to leave. They were born to fly, born to soar. And so are you!

In times of depression your life may feel broken to pieces, yet God can use this experience to give you what you need to become all you were meant to be.

Guard me always as the apple of your eye.

30

A Deep Pilgrimage of Faith

> To provide for those who mourn in Zion—
>   to give them a garland instead of ashes,
> the oil of gladness instead of mourning,
>   the mantle of praise instead of a faint spirit.
> They will be called oaks of righteousness,
>   the planting of the LORD, to display his glory.
>
> ISAIAH 61:3

What's next? Many wonder about this when the doldrums of depression begin to lift. For some, depression could one day dissipate and never return, while for others, the seasons of despondence might recur throughout life.

In either case, we can learn to see how the dark places have led us on a deep pilgrimage of faith. Where we thought we had failed, we have begun, at least in some small way, to fly. We can marvel at where the journey has taken us. We can recognize that, although depression is part and parcel of living, the fragility of our humanness has brought to our days not only ashes but beauty. Through the courageous steps we take to believe, our mourning changes into dancing. In some mysterious way, through all we have suffered, we have been anointed with the oil of gladness. Once faint of spirit, we now sing our praise to God, who displays his glory in us. Though we may still consider ourselves feeble, we are strong. In our very lives, the promises of God have been revealed.

Lord, may we walk together into whatever the future brings.

Prayers

Breath Prayers

When it seems impossible to sit still and prayer is elusive, when you can't sleep at night or you just need a lifeline to God to keep you going through the day, these short prayers can be said in coordination with your breath.

I breathe in Light and breathe out sorrow.
Jesus is with me.
God, give me joy again.
God, come to my assistance. O Lord, make haste to help me.
Jesus, Son of God, have mercy on me.
Do not be afraid, you are mine.
Lord, you are greater than all my sorrow.
Jesus, I trust in you.
Lord, you are close to the brokenhearted.
Lord, accomplish in me yourself everything that you desire of me.

Prayer of Trust

You, O my God, are always thinking of me. You are within me . . . around me. . . . My name is written on the palm of your hand. May I always and in all things do your will.

Lord, I abandon myself in you and relinquish all worry. I abandon myself completely in you, always.

My God, I want to be hidden in you, to lose myself in you, like a drop of water in the ocean.

Venerable Thecla Merlo, FSP

The Memorare

Remember, O most gracious Virgin Mary, that never was it known that anyone who fled to thy protection, implored thy help, or sought thy intercession was left unaided. Inspired with this confidence, I fly unto thee, O Virgin of virgins, my Mother. To thee do I come, before thee I stand, sinful and sorrowful. O Mother of the Word Incarnate, despise not my petitions, but in thy mercy hear and answer me. Amen.

Hail, Holy Queen

Hail, holy Queen, Mother of Mercy, our life, our sweetness, and our hope! To thee we cry, poor banished children of Eve. To thee we send up our sighs, mourning and weeping in this valley of tears. Turn then, most gracious advocate, thine eyes of mercy toward us, and after this our exile, show unto us the blessed fruit of thy womb, Jesus. O clement, O loving, O sweet Virgin Mary.

To My Guardian Angel

Angel of God, my guardian dear,
to whom God's love commits me here,
ever this day be at my side
to light and guard, to rule and guide. Amen.

Psalm 116

I love the LORD, because he has heard
  my voice and my supplications.
Because he inclined his ear to me,
  therefore I will call on him as long as I live.
The snares of death encompassed me;
  the pangs of Sheol laid hold on me;
  I suffered distress and anguish.

Then I called on the name of the Lord:
"O Lord, I pray, save my life!"
Gracious is the Lord, and righteous;
our God is merciful.
The Lord protects the simple;
when I was brought low, he saved me.
Return, O my soul, to your rest;
for the Lord has dealt bountifully with you.

Psalm 116:1–7

Psalm 86

Incline your ear, O Lord, and answer me,
for I am poor and needy.
Preserve my life, for I am devoted to you;
save your servant who trusts in you.
You are my God; be gracious to me, O Lord,
for to you do I cry all day long.
Gladden the soul of your servant,
for to you, O Lord, I lift up my soul.

Psalm 86:1–4

An Ancient Celtic Blessing

You are the peace of all things calm.
You are the place to hide from harm.
You are the light that shines in the dark.
You are the heart's eternal spark.
You are the door that's open wide.
You are the guest who waits inside.
You are the stranger at the door.
You are the calling of the poor.
You are the light, the truth, the way.
You are my Savior this very day.

Wisdom from Saint Teresa of Avila

Let nothing disturb you,
Let nothing frighten you,
All things pass.
God never changes.
Patience obtains all things:
The one who has God lacks nothing.
God alone suffices.

Saint Teresa of Avila

I Believe

I believe, God,
though I cannot see
or hear or feel your presence.
I believe and I trust.
You are the very life within me:
my breath, my heartbeat.
You are within, near me in my pain
    and my emptiness,
my void.
I believe.
Open my heart to gratitude
so that my pain and my emptiness
may be fruitful,
that my darkness may be a creative space
where I come to know you in a new way,
deep and intimate,
deeper and more real than words or images.
And with an open heart
may your stillness and peace and faithfulness
pour out of my being to others.
In the name of Jesus.
Amen.

Maire nic Dhia

Rituals

- ◊ Keep a favorite picture of Jesus close to you where you can see it often.
- ◊ Hold on to a holy card during the long nights when you can't sleep.
- ◊ Hold a rosary in your hands.
- ◊ When you are walking say to God: With every step I renew my trust.
- ◊ Sit in the sun and absorb the light and the warmth. Imagine yourself being surrounded and permeated with God's love.
- ◊ Wear a medal of Jesus or Mary.
- ◊ Keep holy water in your house and use it often for a simple blessing.
- ◊ Listen to Christian music to lift your spirits.

Pauline
BOOKS & MEDIA

A mission of the Daughters of St. Paul

As apostles of Jesus Christ,
evangelizing today's world:

We are CALLED to holiness
by God's living Word and Eucharist.

We COMMUNICATE the Gospel message
through our lives and through all
available forms of media.

We SERVE the Church
by responding to the hopes and needs
of all people with the Word of God,
in the spirit of St. Paul.

For more information visit us at:
www.pauline.org